READING

Edited by Simon Harwin

First published in Great Britain in 1999 by
POETRY NOW YOUNG WRITERS
1-2 Wainman Road, Woodston,
Peterborough, PE2 7BU
Telephone (01733) 230748

HB ISBN 0 75430 341 1
SB ISBN 0 75430 342X

FOREWORD

This year, the Poetry Now Young Writers' Kaleidoscope competition proudly presents the best poetic contributions from over 32,000 up-and-coming writers nationwide.

Successful in continuing our aim of promoting writing and creativity in children, each regional anthology display the inventive and original writing talents of 11-18 year old poets. Imaginative, thoughtful, often humorous, *Kaleidoscope Reading* provides a captivating insight into the issues and opinions important to today's young generation.

The task of editing inevitably proved challenging, but was nevertheless enjoyable thanks to the quality of entries received. The thought, effort and hard work put into each poem impressed and inspired us all. We hope you are as pleased as we are with the final result and that you continue to enjoy *Kaleidoscope Reading* for years to come.

CONTENTS

The Poems

WHO AM I?

I crawl around, looking for food.
Some people are scared of me,
they jump on chairs and scream.

People think my favourite food is cheese,
it's not, I prefer fruit cake
and lots and lots of water.

I've featured in many cartoons
But none of them are true
they make me look like a monster.

My tail's nice and long,
and my eyes are always wide open;
watching out for cats.

Who am I?
Who am I?

Steven Myles (12)

THE WHITE HUNTER

As stealthy as a cat
Trying to catch a mouse
The hunter creeps
from its snowy house.

Searching for food
Over the frozen ground
He sniffs for salty seals
But nothing can be found.

Suddenly he smells a seal!
And starts to dig a hole
Sharp claws slashing and thrashing
Digging like a mole.

Then the seal got away the
Hunter thought maybe another day!

James Purchase (12)

My Mystery Creature

It makes very large sounds,
When it walks on the ground.

It's got lion-like teeth and a very large snout,
It eats fish and meat as it wanders about.

Big boned and a brutal creature,
It's big, green body is its surprising feature.

Eyes like knives and jaws like steel,
A really red raven was its last meal.

The country it lives in is warm and hot,
Rivers and canals are its location spot.

It hunts and it wanders at night,
Looking for a creature to fight.

It is scaly, green and is 20 feet long,
A huge toned creature that is big and strong.

Jamie Webb (12)

WHO AM I?

I slither, slide and glide, no prisoners I take,
My home is the long green reeds by the lake.
Vibrant colours, and pencil sharp teeth,
As deadly as a sword unsheathed.
I'm evil and deadly with my boot black eyes,
As I go skimming, gracefully, elegantly by.
I spring at my prey, as quick as a dart,
I devour it as rapidly as a beat of a heart.
My tongue is as twisted and tangled as wire,
My eyes glow bright with a deadly fire.
I am full now, my skin, stretched and taut,
I can slowly relax, the battle has been fought.
I'm back in the reeds, the earth warms me as I lay,
As I prepare for night and the end of the day.

Emma Rigby (12)

My Mystery Animal

He's as gentle as a dancer
As gentle as a kitten
Diving and jumping,
Swimming in the sea.
His tail is like a mermaid's tail
He's longer than a bus.
As peaceful as a bird in flight.
Communicates with sea life.
And looks a bit like a fish (but bigger)
He prances beneath the sea
And feels a bit like rubber.
He's a nice smoky-grey colour
Just like an elephant, but more graceful
He's so rare and very beautiful.

Louise Wheeler (12)

HALLOWE'EN

H allowe'en is supposed to be scary
A nd about vampires, ghosts and witches.
L ately things have been going weird.
L ast night I felt very light, then I realised I was floating
O n the night of Hallowe'en I wasn't scared at all,
W hen suddenly there was a huge bang.
E veryone in my house went stone-cold.
E verything stopped not a movement to be heard then a
N asty vampire came in the room but it was only my sister
going to a party.

Amy Heath (13)

Spring

Spring's here again with a bang,
Birds are angels enchanting the blue sky
with their beautiful singing,
Sun is booming brightly like a gold doubloon,
Its gold beauty is blessing the daffodils with magic,
The grass is as green as the greenest clover,
Bees are buzzing from flower to flower,
Spring, a time of joy for everyone in the world.

Liam Shurvill (13)

WINTER

Snow covered the ground
like fluffy feathers.
Bald trees hold a sprinkle
of snowflakes
Cold air surrounded the village
like arms made of steel.
Inside people's homes,
fire burned like bonfires.
While they sit around
with hot drinks
children tucked up
snug in bed
Special things they dream of
in their heads.

Laura Wise (13)

HALLOWE'EN

The witches come out on this night,
When the moon is out,
They fly about,
And go sailing past each sleeping house,
Where the pumpkins sleep out like a light,
Down below the children sleep,
Dreaming of their lovely candy they long to eat,
Just earlier in the evening,
There were children everywhere,
The door feeling pain as each child knocks,
Asking for their candy canes,
But now they sleep like sleeping beauty
As the witches slither by,
Making a lot of cackling noises,
But now they disappear,
Just as dawn appears.

Clare Thatcher (14)

Is Something There?

Standing
Still
Its big eyes ever alert.

Antlers
quivering
in the cold night air.
Scratching with his hooves.

Eating
grass and leaves from trees
then chomping ever watchful.

Silently it slips away
not knowing it was there
its brown coat shimmers
in the damp night air.

William Headland (12)

Bang, Bang, Bang

Ears as big as cymbals
A nose like a hose pipe

Feet like drums, *bang, bang*
Bang giving tourists a fright

Eyes as big as golf balls
A mouth like a dustbin truck

A body as dusty and dirty
As it could get slugging
through piles of muck

A belly as big as a garden shed
A tail like a whip

Now this animals arrives at
The water hole as there is
Nothing like a dip.

Charlie Gingell (12)

BERTIE

For a dare,
I proudly sit on Bertie,
Who sniffles and snorts and is rather dirty,
His tatty old clothes are torn,
As he's been standing in the long corn,
His turnip nose is nasty and raw,
And his wig is made of straw,
Patches cover the holes in his ill-fitting tunic,
Bought for a bargain at the local market,
He can't scare a fierce-looking cat
Not even a big, fat rat,
He just shivers and shakes all day long,
As I proudly sit on my friend 'Bertie'.

Cherry Andrews (12)

The Curious Creature

It crawled curiously along the carpet,
Chasing the curious smell.
Its eyes sparkled like rubies, scanning the area,
As its tail waved back and forth, like a long, red snake.
It scuttered along the blue carpet, which looked like a lake.
It sniffed again, smelling the sensational smell.
It ran past the cat and the hair gel.
Its body looked like a gold ball,
As it scuttered down the hall.
Finally it had reached the kitchen,
From where the sensational smell had been coming from.
It looked up and saw the yellow block of excellence.
It ran up the long metal pole,
To finally reach its goal.

George Swain (12)

THE ORANG-UTAN

Orange and hairy
Big and lumpy
Fat and glary
They're like humans
They are apes
They have long arms
They are jungle men
Like 'Orrible old Oscar who eats oranges
And sleeps in a nest of sticks in the trees.
They eat and smile
And walk and swing
They grow up to five feet
And are sometimes known as
Pongo pygmaeus.

Rebekah Carvill (12)

My Pet Peter

Peter's as white a cotton wool,
And has a tail like it too.
Running like a rocket round and round in rings,
He's lightning in a storm.
Ears all long and tall
He bounces like a ball
A nose wet and pink
And beady eyes like marbles
He's really, really sweet
And kind and gentle too.
His nose moves when he eats.
He eats like a pig, rather than who he really is,
And at the end of the day Peter's all mine
And he'll be mine for a very long time.

R Ashton (13)

Pond Dweller

He's slippery and slimy like a slug that's cold
Which makes this creature hard to hold.
He is green as grass
And hard to see as you walk past.
He loves to eat passers-by
And is very fond of an innocent fly.
By ponds and rivers and wet ground
Is where this creature can be found
He does enjoy the occasional soak
And has a rather funny croak
He likes to sit on a lily pad
Still as a statue, looking sad
He leaps and hops with his legs like springs
He really is a funny thing.

Jenna North (12)

DAVID SEAMAN

Rushing off his line, diving at players' feet knowing
there's a risk of getting hurt,
Reaching at full stretch to tip of the ball over the crossbar.
In despair when the ball hits the net,
Pushing the ball with the soft latex on his gloves,
Diving to stop the opponents scoring,
And tipping the ball round the white metal post.
Hear the crowd cheer when he saves a penalty,
Hear the crowd sob when he lets one in.

Steven Horne (11)

Rolo!

Rolo is my pet guinea pig,
He's round and chubby,
He's short and fat,
But I love him
Just like that!

Rolo is my pet guinea pig,
He might be fat and chubby,
But boy is he *fast!*

Rolo is my pet guinea pig,
His fur is white,
With a black stripe,
He might be fat,
But I don't care!
Because I love him the way he is!

Chris Powell (11)

WINTER IS COMING!

Winter is coming to haunt us,
His cold frosty fingertips poised
The gentle scatter of snow covering
                                the ground like skin
The bare oak trees swaying in unison
Icicles form upon the rivers
The animals' dens are full of shivers
All is silent and deprived
He has arrived.

Susan Gregory (14)

Jack Frost - Good or Evil?

The snow fell like frosted flakes,
From the grey sky above.
Jack Frost as icy as the coldest day.
In the chilly morning air,
He danced around the park,
He moved about, light as a feather,
The ground became icy,
Whispering trees, stood in the breeze,
Hung with icicles.
The park, a crystal snow palace,
The iced over lake glistened
In the early morning sunlight.

As Jack Frost left
I walked along
Wrapped up.
Snug as a bug in a rug,
Hat, scarf and gloves
Still, I felt the chill
The sun rose higher
Though it gave no warmth
The snow began to melt
I walked home
The firelight flickered
I felt warm all over
Although I could imagine
The cold outside.

Sarah Polaszewski (13)

WINTER

The snow was falling heavily,
It had a soft feel,
I looked around, the moon was still,
An icy wind blew past me,
I knew that winter had come early.
Fog covered the distance, so it was hard to see,
The streetlights glowed on top of me.
My footsteps crunched across the snow,
Leaving a trail of slush below.
The clouds above covered the moon,
I knew it would be morning soon.
The falling snow turned into sleet,
Which left small puddles around my feet.

Then as I was on my way back home,
The sun broke free, and started to roam,
It made the snow glisten,
And the birds started to sing.
So then I knew a cold winter's morning
Was about to begin!

Clare Prior (13)

Zo-Bo

When he was a kitten he fell over,
Now he flops,
When he was a kitten he yelped,
Now he miaows,
When he was a kitten he chased his tail,
Now he chases mice.

He rubs his face on the corner of my glasses,
His fur makes my skin feel soft and warm,
He follows me to get a stroke
But when he gets one you can never get away.

Zoe's a creamy colour and his fur is as soft as silk,
He love his chest and paws being stroked
Sometimes I call him Zo-Bo!

Sam Hodges (12)

A Special Sister

The minute I was born
I knew she'd be there
As long as I would need her,
Everything, we would go through
It would probably be *together*
From all problems
To going out shopping!
She would be there.

When I need some help
Anyway, anywhere, everywhere
That's where she will be,
Trying to help me.

She comes home with amazing fur coats (very expensive)
And leather mini skirts
And when she's just about to go out clubbing she looks amazing!
She's a very special sister.

Rachel Pollard (11)

WINTER!

Winter is a time for the
Foolish, frosty, figure to come out and scare,
It's here, there and everywhere.

People in their cosy warm homes
Mum's and dad's on their phones,
And children throwing stones.

The frost comes out with the snow,
And forces people to go.

Hurry, hurry, come on, quick.
The frost and the snow are coming,
So be quite slick.

Dogs are barking, cats are miaowing,
And the sky's totally frowning.

So many people are in the streets,
Gangsters how stupid, they're eating sweets!

Trees and plants covered with slimy, slippery snow,
Blimey! the temperature is getting low.

Slowly everybody is in their home
Snug in their beds, the world is completely frozen
and everything is still.

Charlotte Drake (13)

AUTUMN!

The leaves are brown,
And the trees are bare.
The way that the leaves fall off the trees
So lightly floating in the air -
Is like the cold wind being blown
So gently from the clouds,
The cold air clinging to my neck.

Deborah Stace (13)

The Rabbit

There's a woman walking
down the street who trips
over her two left feet.
She stumbles and mutters a
bit of slang and lands with
an almighty bang.
She gets up and stumbles
still and stops
to take a headache
pill
She goes into a butcher's shop and
buys a two pound rabbit chop.
With elegance she strides away and
stumbles as she starts to sway.
She cooks the rabbit until it's tender
and puts it in the electric blender.
She pours it out and mutters still and puts
it on the window sill.
She pours it on to her dinner and says
that rabbit was a winner.

Nicola Wiggins (13)

WAR

Death is common in this place,
Death, like a mouth swallowing up all people,
Swallowing them up in the chaos,
As machine guns fire away,
And with deafening explosions everywhere,
And bullets sailing through the air,
Each death hurting the earth itself.
Then one object falls from the sky,
Falling peacefully like a leaf from a tree,
That one thing will end it all,
A nuclear missile
Will end it all,
Then it hits.
It's all over now,
The battle finishes as quickly as the blink of an eye,
The bodies incinerated in the inferno,
It's over just like that.

Ben Papandreou (13)

Christmas Time

Carollers coming hear their joyful
Singing from all around.

You look in through the window everyone
Is cheerful and merry like a little
Child in a sweet shop, the fire is on.
The tree is lit, the decorations sparkle in
The light.

You wake up, open the curtains
The crisp white of the lawn hits you
The snow has fallen for the first time.

A little robin walking around,
You can see the footprints
In the snow like
Footprints in the sand.

Laura Jones (14)

CHRISTMAS EVE

I love Christmas Eve,
With the carollers walking down
The street like a gaggle of geese,
Singing beautifully,
And the noisy children playing
Excitedly in the snow.

Inside, the fire blaring with a
Fantastic glow as though a fiery
Red flower flying in the wind.

As it grows darker and darker
By the minute,
Everyone surrounds the tree with
A steamy cup of hot chocolate.

It's bedtime now and Santa
Will be on his way,
I lay my head on my pillow and
Hear the sound of jingles nearby
Like sleigh bells on a reindeer.

I closed my eyes,
And whispered, 'Goodnight, goodnight.'

Emma Randall (13)

Hallowe'en

On Hallowe'en everything's a scream,
Trick or treaters knocking on your door,
Scary costumes, ghosts and other things,
Little children saying 'Trick or treat.'

Hallowe'en parties, where every teenager goes,
Everybody in towns celebrating Hallowe'en,
Except for some of those religious guys,
Who don't believe in celebrating Hallowe'en.

On Hallowe'en night everybody's having nightmares,
Dreaming about being scared to death.
They wake up the next morning very tired,
But they don't have to worry, it's half term.

Andrew Brazier (12)

The Mummy

Walking through the passages,
The pyramid is dark,
All by myself,
No one else around,
I hear footsteps coming,
A dark shadow appears.
Moaning as it walks,
Trailing its bandages,
It's coming to get me,
I try to run,
It grabs me . . .
The Mummy - monster of the pyramid.

Hayley Kemp (12)

HALLOWE'EN NIGHT

H allowe'en night is here,
A night of magic, terror and fear,
L ook out for vampires or should I say bats
L isten for the werewolves, devils and rats.
O uiga boards, black magic could ruin your life,
W itches and zombies, killers and their knives.
E erie sounds, spirits, shadows and a full moon
E veryone could be threatened by the voices of doom.
N ever leave your house without a crucifix or salt
people who are killed never know it's their fault!

Charlotte Turner (12)

I'M GOING TO GO OUT ON HALLOWE'EN NIGHT

I'm going to go out on Hallowe'en night,
I'm going to walk the streets and give the guys a fright.
I'm going to dress up on Hallowe'en night,
I'm going to knock on the door and look scary in the light.
I haven't decided what I'm going to wear,
Or what colour to dye my hair.
I haven't decided who I'm going to scare,
I haven't decided who or where.
Maybe I could dress up like a zombie,
Or maybe like a mummy.
Whatever I choose,
I've got nothing to lose
So I'm going to go out on Hallowe'en night,
I'm going to go out looking for a fright.

Steven Turner (12)

TRICK OR TREAT!

The bare trees wave in front of the full moon,
A nightingale screeches off in a deserted castle,
As I walk through the streets with my friends,
A little boy dressed as a ghost jumps out at us.
We knock on a door and shout 'Trick or treat!'
And give us some chocolate and sweets
Shadows are looming
And cackles are booming
As I run home through the night!

Lauren Dewar (12)

A MIDNIGHT FRIGHT

Dark woods, tall trees, never-ending winding paths,
No light at the end of the tunnel .

Steadily walking, nervous, unsure of surroundings,
Crazy howls of werewolves, witches flying above.

Shadows looming,
Poltergeists booming,
Needing to escape this frightful place.

Screeching owls and bats with fangs,
Mummy walking stiffly, bandages on his hands.

This is such a midnight fright - hold on tight.

Rebecca Bennett (12)

Hallowe'en Night

Walking down the street,
Chanting, 'Trick or treat.'
Horror in the air,
Little children everywhere.
Here is a house,
With a pumpkin at the door.
Ask for some sweets
But they don't have any more.

Next is the house,
With a woman living there,
I think she is a witch
With no teeth and no hair.
We knock on the door,
Shout, 'Trick or treat.'
And slowly she says
'Please come in and eat.'
We go into the kitchen and quickly
  take a seat.
Maybe she is not a witch,
Just look at all these treats.
Then she runs out and locks the door
And we're stuck here for evermore.
Ashley, Scott, Denise and I
We all sit down and start to cry.
It's getting dark and very cold
Must we stay here until we're old.
When we're old and die we'll know.
Where that crazy witch did go.

Sarah Walton (13)

Hallowe'en

H anging pumpkins with scary faces cut out,
A scary monster makes a *trick or treater* shout.
L ots of things happen on Hallowe'en night,
L ike witches and vampires give children a fright,
O r mummies and ghosts that knock on your door,
W hen you open it up you give sweets or more,
E very year this night comes around,
E very time scary costumes are found,
N ever get scared on Hallowe'en night.

Ben Cross (12)

I Should Like To . . .

I should like to grasp that minute on every birthday
When out come all the presents.
I should like to smell the TV
But not on animal programmes,
'Cos of all that smell.
I should like to eat the stars,
All the constellations would see my insides
I should like to hear the flowers,
I wonder what they'll say?
I should like to see the wind,
What would it look like?
But if I could do these things,
Or at least in my dreams,
Others would find me crazy,
But I still . . .
Should like to do all the strange, mad things.

Kirstie Lainsbury (12)

WINTER NIGHT

The wind blew up a terrible frost,
As the leaves fell off the trees.
The pond turned to ice,
In the mysterious darkness of the winter night.
The clouds separated to reveal a full moon,
Where the fox hound howled solemnly.
As snowflakes fall to the ground without a sound,
Floating, drifting, like a dream.
In the darkness, in a corner,
A shadow lurks to take the summer away,
Until next year.
Night wanders down a snow blanketed street,
Snow still falling,
In its silent way.

Lisa Jackson (11)

THINK ABOUT POLLUTION!

The main source of destruction
rises into the innocent cloud.
Evilness and carelessness emerges
into the midst of the hills.
Miserable life was what people
called nature.

Passionate lives of
living things being destroyed.
The cloud moves step by step,
river by river, hill by hill,
Life by life. Flowers are
no longer smiling but frowning
with utmost pain.

Grass is no longer a provider
but an innocent murderer in the trance
of a ruined source of nature.
The meaning of life does not
simmer any longer. It slowly
increases into the darkness
of a drifting never-ending death,
causing people to live in
discomfort and despair. The cloud
is kidnapping the youthful vitality
of happy children.

It is hard to believe that
this could be a threat to nature.
But is the cloud the source of evil
it carries, or is it innocent?
Who or what causes the cloud
to put life at risk?

Sophia Nomvete (13)

CHOCOLATE

Chocolate is yum lovely and thick
It cheers you up when you're feeling grim.
Chocolate makes people guilty
but it doesn't stop it being yummy.
Chocolate, chocolate the love of my life
I hate it when you leave my mouth.

Kerry George (13)

HALLOWE'EN

One bitter, foggy Hallowe'en night,
My friends and I were in for a fright.

Looking up at the dark, gloomy sky,
The air is creepy, my oh, my.

We come to the first house on the old street,
Ready to shout, 'Trick or treat!'

The door creeks open but no one is there,
Now we're getting really scared.

By now we are screaming and running back home,
When I trip over a garden gnome.

A cold hand grabs me and turns me around
By now I'm lying on the ground.

Oh look it's just Billy, he's our friend,
I'm glad that this day has come to an end.

Katy Greenway (13)

Hallowe'en

People dress up everywhere,
with funny costumes and purple hair.
People as witches with hats like cones,
and people as skeletons with glowing bones.
Witches with brooms flying in the sky,
and one child shouts, 'There's Mum flying by.'
At the end of the night when the moon is bright,
all the children are in bed wetting themselves with fright.

Amanda Hawker (12)

CHRISTMAS

It's Christmas Eve,
The stockings are out,
I wonder if Santa's about.

We have left the milk and the carrots,
We are now getting ready for bed,
Getting ready to rest our sleepy heads.

It's now Christmas Day,
I'm opening my presents
The moon is still out and it's a crescent.

We're having our dinner,
It's all nice and yum
I wonder if my mum's drinking rum.

Kayleigh Robertson (12)

Anger

Anger is an emotion, the strongest of the lot,
If anger was a colour it would be a dull, dark red.
Anger is an emotion, the fastest of the lot.
It can come and go before you notice the difference.
If anger was an animal it would be a large, dark, domineering but rabid lion.
Strong, powerful, the king of the beasts, like anger is the king of emotions.
If anger was an object it would be a rock,
Strong and simple but also dangerous.
If anger was a food it would be rancid butter,
Horrible, bitter and revolting, making your stomach turn.
If everyone gave into anger, the world would be forgotten.

Daryl Boxall (12)

HALLOWE'EN

It's Hallowe'en and I'm looking for a fright,
I'm dressed up as a vampire and I'm scary in the light.

I have bright white fangs and I'm dressed up in a cape,
I have jet-black hair and my brother's dressed in tape. (He's a mummy)

I knock on the door and there is a pumpkin on the floor,
I say, 'Trick or treat,' and they say. 'Would you like a sweet?'

I close my eyes and I delve in deep,
I suddenly pick up some Quality Street.

After a while I call it a day,
I walk back home and this is what I say:

Hallowe'en
It's a night for a
Fright!

Chris Wells (12)

THE FUTURE

The future world is hard to see
But this is what it is to me.
A world that's run by robots and cars,
Where streets are filled with pubs and bars.
Where robbers and murderers roam the streets,
Jumping out on anyone they meet.
On the other hand it could be nice
Were people like rats and mice
And other creatures like lizards and bugs
And when people greet you they give you big hugs.
Where cars don't speed and zoom
When crossing the road you don't meet your doom.
When children run down grassy hills
Picking up the daffodils.
Wouldn't this world be really good
If it wasn't for criminals it really would.

Lizzie Longmate (13)

FIREWORK NIGHT

Firework night is brilliant,
Beautiful colours sprayed all over the skies.
Jumping Jacks and Catherine wheels,
Bonfires burning Guys.

Children waving sparklers,
And spelling out their names,
Parents organising firework parties,
And playing childish games.

Toasting marshmallows on the bonfire,
Until they drip off the stick,
Children getting excited,
Whilst their mothers are losing their wits.

Rhiannon Rees (12)

One Night In A Year

This is the scariest night in the year,
It always has a feeling of fear,
Trick or treating down your street,
Scary houses, lots of sweets,
Watching scary films at home,
Sometimes you wish that you weren't alone,
You don't want the character to open the door,
But they still do and you watch some more,
Feeling sick after eating the sweets,
Small children scared for weeks and weeks,
On the 1st November the excitement goes,
The witches, the vampires the silly clothes,
You wish it could be every day,
You wait a year and it soon goes away,
I'm sure you've guessed it by now,
The full moon and when the werewovles howl . . .
Hallowe'en!

Samantha Povey (13)

Sailors' Shantys

Pull on the sheets
Tug on the tiller
Start up the engine
Make sure you've filled 'er.

Leave the port
Out to sea
All the halyards
Don't matter to me.

All I care about
Is the sea and the shore
I'll go for a day's sailing
Or more and more .

Cross the oceans
In a Chinese junk
I saw the Titanic
When it sunk.

I've seen many'a sailor
Make a silly mistake
'Man overboard.'
Left in our wake.

A silly sailor
Is no use to his crew
He wastes all the gin
And eats all the stew.

Michael Stebbings (12)

Guy Fawkes' Night

Going around in the middle of the night,
Unsurprisingly he's carrying dynamite,
Sneaking around in the middle of London,
The Government house could be no more,
Waiting around until the time is right,
Striking from the darkness,
Pushing the handle down,
But this is just a dream,
For the police are around,
Waiting to catch Guy Fawkes out,
Bang! Went the dream. *Banged-up!* Was the reality.

Steven Thomas

Hallowe'en Night

It was a dark night,
the full moon was half covered by a cloud.
The frosty air sent icy chills down the devils' backs.
The witches cackled their evil laughs.
The skeleton's dark-ringed eyes
stared at the zombies and demons
as they walked through the graveyard.
The pumpkins' shadows danced as the candlelight flickered.
Everything seemed so real
but it was only a Hallowe'en party
decorated as an eerie graveyard.
The dancing zombies, demons, devils,
witches, ghosts and monsters
seemed so real,
but they were only costumes
which would be put away for next year.

Rebecca Bramall (12)

On The Night Of Hallowe'en

It had just turned dusk,
Everyone started coming out,
All in different costumes,
No faces to be seen.

Painted faces,
Ugly costumes,
Witches, ghosts, werewolves,
Vampires, devils and candlelight.

Knocking on doors, not knowing
If they want a treat or have done a trick.
No one knows
'Cause they're very quick.

Black magic is quite scary,
Ouija boards, curses,
A great big spell book,
That's what the witches did.

Haunted houses,
With flying bats,
Lots of pumpkins,
Monsters and all that.

Next morning, everything is
Back to normal.
Gone to work, now waiting
For next Hallowe'en to come.

Natalie Canham

In The Garden

The sun is bright up in the sky
and lots of flowers on the ground
I'd like to be a buzzing bee, to fly
to collect my nectar from all around.

The birds are singing in the trees
and butterflies are fluttering
Out in the garden my brother and me
but he just will not stop muttering.

The green green grass
is full of creepy crawly ants
I don't like to sit down
in case they get in my pants.

There's a frog in the pond
he goes *croak croak croak*
We have quite a bond
the name I call him is Oke doke.

Helen Quelch (11)

My Hallowe'en Acrostic!

H allowe'en is such a treat
A ll the kids get lots of sweets
L ove dressing up and having fun
L ooking ugly and sticking out their tongues
O ver-excited with candy and money
W itches with warts and starry-eyed zombies
E veryone's happy and laughing together
E veryone's parents are handing out their money
N o one's empty-handed, their bags are full of treats.

Lucy Gladwell (12)

Happy

Happy sounds like laughter
Happy looks like fun
Happy feels nice
Happy tastes like McDonald's
Happy is good.

Dean Carrick (12)

HAPPY

Happy looks like the sun
Happy sounds like the birds
Happy feels like the sand
Happy tastes like roast dinner
Happy tastes like McDonald's
Happy feels like you're on holiday
Happy sounds like the ice-cream van.

Luke Jakalowski (12)

MYSTERY ANIMAL

Skin as shiny as gold
Its colour is very bold
If I was to break my tail
I would begin to wail
If my mummy's home began to mould
It would become very cold
Sometimes we live with snails
But we never ever live with quails
We live at the back of a house which has been sold
And my grandad is growing old
My first name is dale
My last name is bail
No one can fool me, so my mummy told.

Koren Roberts (12)

SHARK

It stalks you like a cheetah,
It is the ocean's greatest eater.
With a rounded nose that can smell fear,
You don't even know when it is near.

Its streamline shape slides through the secretive sea,
The white death, that is he.
His fin cuts through the sea like a knife,
You never know if he'll take your life.

His dagger teeth, as strong as iron,
He will strike at you like a lion.
His white belly gives him his name,
He will never escape his unwanted fame.

He is a great fisherman's trophy,
But he's not a man-killer, not to me.

Jody Claridge (12)

What Is It?

Its claws are like daggers,
They're ready to stab us,
It's a great big rainbow,
And as strong as a jumbo.
They terrorise the tiny,
Their teeth are very shiny,
Their techniques are tremendous,
They're traditionally horrendous.
it is a big rug,
With its face so smug,
It acts like a beast,
And it always has a feast.
It's all stripey with fur,
As it leaps how it does.

Rachel Bell (12)

WHAT AM I?

Kelly moves across the land
Feet sinking in the sand
Eating leaves and fruit all day
Does she eat meat? No way!

At birth she was baby pink
At first she couldn't blink
In a few days, she could walk
In a few days, she could talk.

Kelly is about 3 feet high
Kelly doesn't know how to cry
Her floppy ears as big as a house
When she was born she was a mouse.

Her long thin nosc like a hose
Kelly will get bigger as she grows.

Laura Park (12)

HALLOWE'EN NIGHT

Tonight's the night it's Hallowe'en,
People frightened as well as the Queen.
Children ready for trick or treat,
Hoping to get a bag of sweets.

Witches are flying out and about,
Making little children shout, shout, shout!
As well as wolves howling at the moon,
Wishing children will come to them soon.

Skeletons and pumpkins hanging from the ceiling,
Most parents have a terrible feeling.
Hoping the children will not be long,
Singing a song, doing nothing wrong.

Getting the children ready for bed,
Then they are waiting to be fed.
Off they go up the stairs,
Snuggle in bed with their blue teddy bears.

Lorna Hutchins (12)

Catz

Wilbur is a podgy cat
And Monty eats plastic,
They clean each other day and night
And cough up hairballs round and tight.
A trip to the vets or cattery,
Almost always proves to be,
Another nasty fight.
But when we come to pick them up,
They're as affectionate as always,
(Content for a while, I hope!)
They go outside,
Find new places,
Chase a bird or two.
They haven't caught one yet thank goodness,
And I hope they never do.

Vikki Lewis (11)

The Hook

The murderer of the depths
just sits there waiting
with maggots and worms
squirming to get off and free.

Then up it comes -
the victim
unsuspecting of its fate
it snaps and is trapped.
The hook is now embedded
maliciously driven into the victim.

Unaware of its actions
it wheels the helpless victim in.
The pathetic crippled victim
is now almost dead

but thinking it's alive
they throw it straight back in.

The mutilated victim just lies there
helplessly, in horrific pain.

The hook has done its job
the victim is destroyed
ripped it up inside
and slaughtered
the innocent victim
then back in goes the hook
to pick off its next victim
just a sport they say. I don't think so.

James Beisly (14)

EXCITED POEM

Excited sounds like the going home bell.
Excited looks like fun.
Excited looks like happiness.
Excited tastes like sweets.
Excited smells like burgers.
Excited is the best thing in the world.

Michael Swain (12)

HATE

Hate sounds like fire
Hate looks like a dark red
Hate feels like sandpaper
Hate tastes like rotten eggs
Hate smells like a toilet
Hate is the worst thing in life.

Damian Cracknell (12)

My Wonderful Nan

My nan is very thoughtful, kind and considerate,
She is helpful, loving and nice,
Even though she is getting older,
Every day she seems to me that her energy
    is slowly drifting away.

I imagine my nan sitting, knitting and thinking
in her favourite chair,
About the different things that are happening all
around her.

Even though my nan's energy is drifting away,
her wisdom is growing and growing,
further and further,
more and more.

Claire Palmer (11)

Mum!

Most of the time she's always there,
giving lots of love and care.

When tears are close, she'll make me laugh -
happy and chatty with a very warm heart!

Problems are solved with her cups of tea -
she's thoughtful and helpful - she's my
Mummy!

Denita Whitelock (11)

BRIAN AND LILLY

Brian and Lilly are really soft and cuddly
Lilly is so perfect, she washes herself wherever she is,
Brian is such an adorable cat,
He sleeps a lot but fun he is and such a handsome chap.

Wherever there is a warm bed, be sure Brian will be there,
Wherever a nice spot is, be sure to see Lilly there.

Rochelle Pentland (11)

Denita

Denita is my friend
Singing, dancing
We're round the bend.

Dancing around up and down,
Singing too it's fun to do.

Laughing at jokes and
making funny sounds
We're really happy in the town.

We meet Rochelle our other friend
and go to the disco which
never ends.

Kimberley Foster (11)

BOUNCER AND ME

Me and Bouncer are best friends,
Running and walking it never ends.

Going for walks in the park. Playing
Around, it's just a laugh.

We love to run and have a laugh.
Having fun we've just begun!

I love you Bouncer!

Nikita Chadda (11)

THE HEREFORD BULL

The Hereford bull's an ugly creature,
The Hereford bull's a friend.
The Hereford bull's a smart creature,
Against him you can't defend.

Out in the field with other cows,
How nicely coloured they are.
If a bull charged at you,
It would leave more than just a scar.

Out in the field where cows play,
They wish that they could stay,
When they go to get milked,
I could watch the Hereford from the hay.

Daniel Cooney (11)

My Hamster, Chubby

My hamster Chubby was a loveable pet,
He had tiny feet,
And lots of soft, smooth hair.

My hamster Chubby was so energetic,
He would run around in his cage,
With such rage.

My hamster Chubby was so snuggly,
He would curl up in your hand,
And fall fast asleep.

My hamster Chubby was my best pal,
And still is now.

My hamster Chubby died in August,
I cried and cried,
I wouldn't eat,
We buried him in the garden.

My hamster Chubby was such a lovable pet.

Laura Makepeace (11)

NIBBLES

My Nibbles is a friendly fish,
I'd never lay her upon a dish.
Nibbles plays, she sucks my finger,
I'd never have her for my dinner.
Nibbles is so very cute,
I wonder if she can play the flute.
Little Nibbles' lips are made for blowing bubbles,
A flute in her lips is sure to bring her troubles.
Nibbles will swim non-stop for day,
But when she sees me she'll know it's time to play.

Tarah Springer (11)

SLEEP

Sleep, I think is a mysterious thing,
Peacefully dreaming until the alarm clock rings,
Dreams are definitely weird as well,
What you dream no one can tell,
When you are asleep, you can't think,
Strange dreams that have no link,
Snuggled up tight, cosy in bed,
Dreaming good things or bad things instead.

Eleanor Davies (11)

WAR

War is a terrible thing.
Fires starting as the bomber planes deposit their bombs,
Leaving a trail of devastation.
The feeling that the next bomb or bullet could be the death of you -
Waking up to find that next door's house is no more,
Instead, lies a twisted piece of metal that used to be a bomb.
Petrified just when you are walking to school.
War is a terrible thing and should not be inflicted on anyone,
Just because of a political argument,
Or, a political leader wanting to get more than is possible.
Greed is a treacherous thing;
So is jealousy;
Because, after all, violence is no way to solve anything.

Matt Stevenson (12)

My Two Brothers

I'm eleven years old and my name is Kelly,
I always sit in front of the telly.
I've got a baby brother, and a big one too,
But I'd rather have a stuffed cockatoo
Darren is thirteen, but more like three,
He definitely acts much younger than me.
He's got no girlfriends, I'm not surprised,
And on his trousers, he's got no flies.
That's enough about him, you think that's bad?
When you see the other one, you'll go mad.
Shane, he scribbles on walls, and paints them too,
And never goes to the toilet in the loo.
When you try to get him dressed,
He is always such a pest.
When you tell him it's time for bed,
He always says he hasn't been fed.
I'm not like them, I'm good as gold,
I'm just like my mum, but not as old.

Kelly Westwater (11)

FOOTBALL

F ootball is the greatest game.
O wen scoring great goals and making
his fame.
O ther players making money out of
a game they love.
T ackles coming in hard and tough
B oys' game only just too rough.
A ll the players doing their best to
score a great goal.
L adies can also play, but make sure
you don't go too rough.
L ots of people play because
it's the best.

Michael Herbert (12)

My Life Is Hell

My life is hell,
After the school bell.
When I walk home
They know I'll be alone
I can hear them talking
But I carry on walking
I can feel them looking at me
Why can't they just let me be?
When I get home Mum won't be there
I know they will get in and run up the stairs.
They will get into my room and throw everything.
If there is anything worth having they will
steal my nan's ring.
I'm sitting in the corner shaking with fear,
Knowing that they will be here.
My life is hell,
There's no one I can tell.
I'm going to try and fight back,
Stop them stealing my rucksack.
Tell them to leave me alone
And stop them getting into my home.
My life should get better
Maybe if I write them a letter.
I can't stand this anymore,
My legs and arms are very sore
Please, please stop this now,
Be nice to people, you should know how.

Tracie Graves (13)

Happiness

Happiness is something money can't buy,
It is something that is stuck inside,
Until you think of something happy,
Just don't think of a mouldy nappy.
You do not need a magic potion,
To use this happy emotion.
It won't run away from inside your heart,
In a little horse's cart.
This is the best emotion,
So come on, and do the Locomotion!

Rebecca Drew (11)

AUTUMN

Leaves falling off the trees,
The wind blowing hard and strong,
Wellies crunching the frost as children
walk to school.

Crunching, crunching, crunching, crunch!

Squirrels snoring in their beds
Dead leaves lying beneath your feet,
Squelching mud from the rain last night.

Crunching, crunching, crunching, crunch!

First snow at the end
Lays white and untouched,
Then footprints appear.

Crunching, crunching, crunching, crunch, crunch!

Amii Barnes (11)

ENJOY SUNDAY DINNER?

I wait, cramped into a small place,
Crushed with many others of my kind.
Restrained by wooden pens,
Enclosed by watchful, glaring walls
Unable to move, flattened by others bigger than me.
Just a mass of writhing wool
Struggling for life.
Waiting.
Helpless to the needles that fill me with fear,
Crippled by the bolts embedded in me,
And tortured by the blasting charges
That end the waiting.

Some time later, a child sitting at the dinner table, asks to be passed the mint sauce. For a minute she pauses.
'Mummy, what's this?'
'It's your dinner, eat up.'
'But what exactly is it?'
'It's lamb. Who wants vegetables?'
'Like the lambs we saw in the field the other day?'
'Gravy anyone?'
'They got killed then?'
'What?'
'The lambs we saw, they got killed. How did they die?'
'Well . . . you don't really want to know.'
'Does it hurt them a lot then? Mummy, you said they were sweet, and now you're eating them.'
'Do you want more vegetables?'
'Did they get killed?'
'No.'
'I'll eat them then.'

Claire Jackson (14)

Jealousy

Jealousy is something deep inside
You don't like to show it because of your pride
It's huge and green.
Dangerous and mean.
Bubbling ready to *pop!*
However hard you try it's something that you
just can't stop!

Jealousy is sour not sweet,
Trust me, it isn't a treat.
It's something you have to live with
There's nothing that anyone can do
You've just got to try your hardest to stop
jealousy getting to you.

Joanne Proudley (11)

HELP!

I was walking home on a cold dark night.
I stopped to do my lace.
I looked in front and then behind
There he was, standing in the rain
Looking cold, dark and evil.
I turned to run,
I heard him behind
Then *c r a s h!*
I had fallen over my lace.
He reached out to grab me,
I screamed and yelled.
He covered my mouth.
I tried to get away.
I was alone,
I screamed,
I screamed,
I was dead!

Sam Howe (12)

ALIENS

Aliens are everywhere,
Living under your bed,
You see them in your dreams,
Don't ever be afraid to scream,
You see the aliens flying past,
When you are having a bath,
Now it comes to the end of this scene,
The aliens go off, never to be seen.

Emma Biles (12)

BLACK

Black is scary
Dark as dark
All night long the dogs bark.

Black is funerals
Leading you to trouble
So whenever you see black
Stay out of trouble.

Black are our clothes
Black is on our bags
Black is on our jewellery,
Wherever you go, guess what you see?
Black, black and black!

Jolly Moktadir (12)

MITCH

He's coming closer,
He's trying to ask me something,
I think he's following me,
He's now tugging my shirt,
He wouldn't hurt me,
I think he wants to play,
He's pulling harder and harder
He's so strong,
I can't let go or I'd lose.
Uh oh! I let go,
His tail is wagging with joy,
'I'll get my own back on you'
I tell him.
I don't care, he's my dog,
Called Mitch whom I love to bits,
but I can't say the same about his bone!

Stephanie Prior (13)

My Two Friends!

My tall friend Suzanne Shirley,
Used to live in Purley.
She fell down her stairs,
And broke her mum's chairs.
Now she lives in Ford's Farm,
She is really very calm!

My best friend Lucy is real cool
She even has a swimming pool.
She has a big house,
And a pet mouse
Which she calls Larry!

Teri Whelan (12)

FOOTBALL AND ME

I am a Blackburn supporter,
A Blackburn supporter for long,
I've watched them play,
And win that day,
And that's why I support them.

I play for Westwood Wanderers,
Like when I was eight years old,
I play in mid-field,
And have scored two goals,
And that's why I play for them.

I support Blackburn,
I play for Westwood,
And that's my football life.

Alan Beckford (12)

FRIENDS

F unny friends getting into trouble
R obbing stores for food, *gobble gobble!*
I have an idea, hitch-hike the bus!
E veryone and everyone chasing after us
N ow me and my pals were in a lot of trouble.
D on't tell anyone
S ee you burst our bubble.

Kevin Pitt (12)

THE BULLY

At twelve o'clock I dread to go
into the playground.
People shout and scream and call me
names, they really think they're big!
But then through the crowd I see a head
going up and down, things run through
my head, I know that that's the bully.
He comes closer and closer and isn't
going to stop, he's running now, really fast,
I try and get away but people grab my arm
really tight and *thump!* I get it in the arm,
I squeal and squirm and then get away,
but I know he will get me another day.

Laura Hunt (12)

PREDATORS OF THE WILD

The safety lock hooked back,
The rifle aimed to deliver one mortal blow,
The poacher brings his baneful eye down to meet the sight,
His eye locks upon his target,
Just 50 metres away,
Lies his next victim.

The lion perched on a soft-grained rock,
Flicking its untamed ears back and forth,
Not knowing that soon, life will be gone.

The poacher takes stance,
As the lions prance,
His finger numb with guilt.
He squeezes his well-trained finger and releases,
Hammering out a virulent bullet,
As it rips the pressured air,
Homing in on its commanded position.

The bullet scorches into the lion's crown, tearing tissue
The lion falls down with an omnipotent roar.

As it lies dead with a crippled head,
The poacher congratulates his gun.

Ricky Goddard (14)

THE WEB WATCHER

As the boss of the web lay still,
The workers kill and bring in a meal.
The female of the species is more
deadly than the male,
And yet, they do not fail.

As the night has come, they need their rest,
As they think that they have done their best,
The lightning strikes and thunder begins,
The spiders begin to hug and cringe.

As morning comes, it is as light as day,
The spiders begin on their way,
A kid comes along and begins to stare,
And he thinks to himself 'Oh my God,
What are they doing there?'

The kid goes away,
And comes back with a spray, he comprehends
They have gone on their way,
He catches them up and showers the spray,
And now he has assassinated them each away.

The insects lay as still as day,
Their life has been taken all away.
The kid comes along with a dustpan and brush,
And carries them to the bin with all of the dust.

Rebekah Thomas (14)

WHO'S THAT NEW GIRL?

Who's that new girl over there?
Just look at her, look at her hair.
Her teeth as white as snow,
And her hair tied up in a pretty pink bow.
Look at her dress, all pretty and neat,
And her tidy shoes on her little feet.
Look at the boys looking her way.
She looks her best every day.
I wish I could be like her.

Aimee Kirkpatrick (12)

THE DOLPHIN AND THE MOON

The dolphin swims alone at night.
The water splashes and turns to Sprite.
The dolphin's name is Lonely Sprite
Because she dances alone at night.

The moon comes up, the dolphin rises,
Her face is full of excitement and surprises.
She jumps across the water,
Her back is arched as well.
The sight is amazing, you cannot miss it.

The dolphin jumps high in the sky, and
Rises above the moon and I.

Emma Parmenter (12)

ORCA

He swims gracefully along
the bottom of the sea,
His tail gently swaying
from side to side,
Every now and again opening
his mouth to gobble down some fish.
He starts to swim to the surface,
breaking up the gentle water and
leaping into the open air.
His body bends and he splashes
back into the water.

Holly Cooper (13)

RABBIT

I'm lying here waiting for the next shock,
All around me I hear the loud screaming
Of friends being hurt.
The constant drone of the drill.

I hear the cage door open.
Two hands reach in and clasp me.
A black sheet is thrust over my head,
I feel myself being tied down,
A paw to each corner.

My ears are pinned back,
Needles are embedded under my skin,
I start to feel terror
But there is no purpose to bellow,
They don't listen.

I'm constantly stabbed and tested on,
I want to give up.
I don't think I can live anymore,
I don't think I want to.

Hayley Monger (15)

A Sad Tail

Bounding across this brown springy place,
Sinking my teeth into a nice piece of wood.
Enjoying myself, just having some fun,
Little did I know the trouble I'd begun.

The door flew open and in he strode,
Took one look around, a pause lasting eternity,
He glared at me, looked me straight in the eye,
Then a lot of garbled shouting ending in a sigh.

After the sigh he disappeared through the door,
But I was pretty sure he would be back once more.
I sat cowering in the corner, feeling cold,
Just wishing the floor would swallow me whole.

Back he came, his face as black as thunder,
Carrying a sack by his side. I was filled with dread.
As he approached me further, I tried to run,
A sharp pain in my side and down it came.

Darkness

As I stirred from my sleep, I was still being carried
Curled in a ball at the bottom of my prison,
Suddenly we stopped and all went quiet,
The sack lifted from beneath me, tumbling around inside.

Shivering, freezing, beginning to go numb,
Choking, spluttering, don't even know what I've done.
Feeling colder still, just wanting to sleep,
Eyelids drooping, can't swim anymore, *tired, tired!*

Darkness!

Joanne Ward (15)

This Little Piggy

I am a piglet
Only one year old
Farmer's coming to get me
Three o'clock I'm told.

My sister went last week
Taken away in farmer's truck
What have I done to
Deserve this bad luck.

Off I go
Being carried away
Never gonna see night again,
Or day.

A long shiny knife
Lying by my side
I was hoping and praying to live,
But I died.

This is my conscience speaking
I'm being laid on a trolley
I've been put next to
A box of lollies!

I'm going across a checkout
Bleep, bleep, bleep!
I'm being put in a bag
With a tonne of leeks.

I'm laid on a table
All cooked and well-done
I've been placed on a fork now
The meal has just begun.

Vicky Reynolds (14)

My Masters Love Me?

My masters love me,
Well I can't complain,
I mean they give me food, water and shelter,
What else could I ask for?

Of course my ears have gone now,
It was my fault really,
I did bark after dark.

My tail has gone now,
That was an accident,
He wouldn't tread on it purposely.

I'm blind as well,
But how could he have known
I was in the way when that bleach was thrown?

Now I only have three legs
That brick was rather heavy

But my masters love me . . . really they do!

Ashley Pearce (14)

ODE TO MR HEDGEHOG

Little beastly hedgehogs so warm and alive,
You have a funny little snout and curl up inside.
With your armour to protect you against any harm,
You're always in danger but always seem so calm.
You have lived a thousand years,
Why so many tears?
Cos, you do not need to battle with or run away from foes,
You just stand and get splattered in the middle of the road.
Do we really aim for you or is it just bad luck,
Or are you just attracted to the lights of a speeding truck?
Poor little hedgehogs where have you all gone?
We don't mean to harm you, when we're driving along.
Do you need protection or some sort of code,
Or do you need your own, special little road?

Victoria Wheeler

THE SNAKE

As the long, smooth, snake slithers through the reeds of the jungle,
The poacher listens, but the snake, she is silent,
She always outsmarts them.

She knows what they're after, it's either her skin or her flesh,
The poachers think that she's dumb,
After all, there's little room for a brain inside her,
But she knows.

She's still, as she waits for him to come near,
He spots her colourful scales glistening in the sun,
She can hear him whisper to himself,
As he takes his last steps towards her.

She remains still as his shadow towers over her,
He has his finger poised on the trigger of his gun,
Ready, set, *aim and . . .*

She digs her crystal-sharp teeth into his leg,
As he collapses to the ground, screaming in pain,
She always outsmarts them.

Sarah Carver (14)

Lion

Crouching, growling, running, waiting
That's a Lion's trade.
The wind sways the grass, then, like a flash of lightning he bolts
and pounces, then *bang!*
The prey runs, startled, the grass is still!

The sound of screeching wheels make us wake from this
sleepy gaze.
As our eyes scour the horizon in search of someone or something
Then finally we see, limping away, the King of the jungle.

The limp gets worse, he can't go on,
But suddenly there *is* a friend, his Lioness appears as if by magic
to help her wounded mate.
But still he falters and finally falls.

The Lioness stands dutifully beside her mate and waits for death's
cold blanket to fall upon his head, as she does so she weeps for
her lost treasure.
The hunters move on, their job is done
They crouch, they run, they wait, they kill
That's the lion trade.

Emma Basden (14)

WHO AM I?

Tearing through the grass,
Who am I?
Entering the house,
Climbing up the tall dark steps
With my eager aim to frighten someone
Who am I?
As I come out of the plug-hole, I reach light at last,
Until a tall, dark, gruesome shadow passed my view.
I see a strange image,
It's that barbaric giant,
As it waves a piece of paper in front of me,
I can see the blood on it now,
I think to myself, you won't catch me.
I'm too fast.
I imagine it catching me and pulling my eight legs off,
One by one.
I hear it singing 1, 2, 3, 4 . . . then it flaps the paper
in front of me.
It's too late, just too late!

Katie Purdy (14)

WHY WON'T THEY LEAVE US ALONE?

Out they come again,
Every night they do.
Hunting for a treat,
Why won't they leave us alone?

Searching by the lapping sea,
Digging in the sand,
Seeking out our shells and eggs,
Why won't they leave us alone?

After our flesh again,
For Chinese remedies and medicines.
Using our shells and skin for
Tourist trade.
Why won't they leave us alone?

They're wiping us out,
We're nearly extinct
Because of their brutal
But deadly fun.
Why won't they leave us alone?

I heard two barbaric creatures
Talking about how to catch
Their next pathetic victim.
I waited with intense frustration,
Knowing I may be the next
Turtle, the next pathetic victim.

Joanne Taylor

As Black As Night

As the dark sky comes,
Dustbin lids rattle, bottles fall to the floor,
As the cat, as black as night, wanders the street,
All alone, nowhere to go.

Roaming the town,
Looking for a quiet place to sleep,
No one to talk to,
No friends, just the enemy of the night,
As the dog in the distance, howls at the moon.

The chase is on, two stray cats run past
The lamp posts flicker,
Scratching, scraping, screeching.
As they fade into the distance,
The black of the night surrounds him again.

As the bright headlights blind him,
He is picked up, thrown into a van,
Locked in a cage,
But the cage is warm and dry,
He is being cared for, he is happy.
The black of the night fades into the distance.

Out of the cage and into a box
approaching the 'Medical Research Centre'
This is not care, this is death
Say goodbye to the black of the night,
Forever.

Kathryn Jarvis (15)

HAPPINESS

Happiness is joyful,
Happiness is making new friends,
Happiness is getting new pets,
Happiness is *Love*
Happiness is eating and drinking,
Happiness is getting a new job,
Happiness means enjoying yourself.

Hayley Bolton (11)

THE FISH'S LAST JOURNEY UPSTREAM

The clear water was cold
As the fish made its way upstream.
This fish had made this journey
Many times before,
But this was to be the last.

It swam hard against the
Strong current of the stream,
Its scales shimmering
In the warm sunlight that
Filtered through the swaying trees.

Suddenly,
The water was disrupted
And mud swirled up from the
Bottom of the once still
Riverbed.

The fish could no longer see where
He was swimming,
And started to panic.
He tried to swim away,
But he found himself caught in a plastic net.

A large hand reached in towards the fish,
And the fish thrashed more.
Panicking, scared, alone.
The fish gasped for air which he couldn't find,
The pain spreading through his small body.

The man put the fish on the floor,
The fish still thrashing wildly.
Slowly, the fish became weak,
Not being able to breathe anymore.
He took his last breath then became still.

Sara Beckett (14)

POEM

As I run through the battlefield
I see the remains of a hundred people
As the person next to me cries out in pain
I think about fear, what is fear?
Fear is the thing that makes children look under
their bed before they go to sleep.
Fear is the black hand that pushes people down in the mud
But my heart was filled with not just fear, but excitement also
But what is excitement?
Excitement is the thing that drives us forward towards our goal
As more people fall and I hear their agonised screams
I think about my family and my friends
I fire from the hip, my hands shaking from the recoil of the gun
Suddenly, I feel a searing pain in my stomach and I fall to the ground
Blood is dripping from the wound and as I lose consciousness, my last
thought is why me, Lord, why me?

Carl Taylor (13)

THE MISUNDERSTOOD LIFE OF AN ANT

I run about knowing what I know,
There is danger all around me.
I have to hang low,
Some dangers are there for all, some you cannot see.

I know one day I will be gone,
Crushed with nothing to leave.
You could say that I had no value to you,
But your ignorance I do not need.

I know you think that we mess around in the dirt,
And steal your food.
But if something were to happen to the Earth
We would be last to leave.

I know it's not long before I die,
Thus ending my insignificant life.
I may not mean much to you,
But to me I mean more than mankind.

Sumran Choudrey (14)

DEAD OR ALIVE

Every second, every hour
Every day and every week
I fly around all day long
Finding things to eat.

I search in people's gardens
In their houses too
All I really want
Is some nice, yummy food.

They hit me with their swatters
I fall down to the floor
My wing has been pulled off
And I can't fly round no more.

They stamp me with their feet
All over my poor head
My brains all fall out
And now I think I'm *dead.*

Leanne Osborne (15)

The Elephant

'Bang, bang, bang!' The gun has spoken,
The Elephant has been awoken
From the daze for which he'd entered,
Came an almighty screech.

The Elephant fell to its knees
And begged the group of poachers, 'Please!'
They stood and watched as his deep blue eyes closed.
They said 'The Elephant just has to go.'

The creature lay on the ground,
He did not move or make a sound.
The Elephant was no more,
He had to go and leave this world.

The poachers stood and listened for a while,
But all they could hear was a crocodile.
They knew he was only a corpse from now on
So they carried on with their quest for his ivory tusks.

Georgina Warwick

ANGER

Anger is red like the colour on our ties,
When the movies aren't on,
When we get homework,
When you can't get into clubs,
When we are behind Sunday drivers,
When my mum or dad tell me off,
When my sister annoys me,
When my friends annoy me,
When my friends don't believe me,
When I get presents that I don't like.

Amanda Jordan (11)

ANGER

Anger is when you reach the phone
Just as it stops ringing
Anger is when a bee hits you
And you can't stop the stinging

When I'm tired it is worse
Anger hits me like a curse

Anger is when you're on the road
People get more cross
Nobody has any patience
They all think they're boss

When I get home, I can't get in
I've lost my key, I just can't win

Anger is when you miss the bus
And the movie starts at three
You can't be late you've got a date
This was your big chance with Lee

It makes me mad when I get blamed
I should have had my sister tamed

Anger is when you get home late
To find the fridge is bare
You're starving and you're thirsty
But there's simply nothing there.

Anger is when you're at the beach
And it begins to rain
You've just set up the deck chairs
Now take them down again

I get angry with my homework
I like to get it right,
Sometimes it takes me ages
I'm up for half the night.

Laura Morgan (11)

Happiness

Yellow and orange are colours of happiness,
Sunrise in the morning,
Summer sun shining all day long,
Long summer evenings and the setting sun.

Yellow and orange are colours of happiness,
Days on the beach in the bright yellow sun,
Floating along rivers, time floating by.
Time to enjoy with my friends and family.

Yellow and orange are colours of happiness,
Bright yellow daffodils coming up into the spring
Orange roses in the summer sun,
These are the things that remind me of happiness.

Charlotte Haas (12)

Sleepy

Lying in bed all nice and warm
Feeling sleepy
Knowing you have to get up for school
Makes the feeling go.

Lying in bed all nice and cosy
Saying to myself 'Do I have to get up?'
But I know I have to.
I jump in the shower to get nice and clean
Then I jump out of the shower feeling refreshed.
I try to find my school clothes
But I remember it's a Saturday!

Lisa Bosley (11)

FEELINGS

Feeling hurt and all alone
finding people hard as stone.

Feeling lost like living in hell
not having someone you can tell.

Living a life through a long black hole
needing a friend to bare your soul.

Having a happy thought or two
when you smile people ignore you.

Life is sorrow pain and shame
will anything be ever better again.

Parents, teachers don't understand
how other children are underhand
with cruel words, acts and deeds,
these bullies will succeed.

Being bullied you detest
getting angry and get stressed.

We all feel happy or sad
in us all is good and bad
perhaps I won't wake tomorrow
and feel this pain and sorrow

But I will brave another day
as the bullies won't get their way.

Steven Coleman (11)

TIME FEELS LIKE FOREVER

Time can seem to last for an eternity,
Or fly by as speedily as a summer's day,
How it does this we cannot see,
To fathom time there is no way.

The seconds seem to feel like forever,
As the years roll by the minutes wander,
Until it starts to seem like never,
Whilst the hours feel even longer.

The decades rush by without a pause,
Yet the weeks seem to cruise casually by,
Each New Year celebrated with just cause,
Yet few seem to ask the reason why.

Time is described as having wings,
A moment slowly comes and quickly goes,
Like an eagle or other such things,
Time can leave us full of happiness or woes.

Twenty-four hours feels like forever,
At times every day is just like another,
Until it's gone to return never,
Time will wait for no other.

Time can pass quickly away,
Ticking by quickly, speedily and soft,
Then that's the end of another day,
Fluttering away like a moth,
Though time can feel like forever.

Danielle Park (13)

LIFE

Life is but a ship,
that sails upon thy shore.
It anchors up and settles,
yet is not one bit distraught.

Life is but a flower,
that blows upon the breeze.
It opens up and closes,
gives pollen to the bees.

Life is but a dream,
it floats into your mind.
Yet in the morning it sails away,
a strange kind of mankind.

Life is but a ship,
that sails upon thy shore.
It anchors up and settles,
yet is not one bit distraught.
Then one day it sails away,
never to return again.
But do not worry as it is always there,
and can sail into thy dream.

Claire Dillon (13)

HALLOWE'EN

H allowe'en night is here once more
A nd trick or treaters are knocking on doors
L ights are out, the houses dark
L adies scream as wild dogs bark
O wls hoot their midnight tune
W itches fly across the moon
E vil wailings give plenty a fright
E veryone is a victim on Hallowe'en night
N ot even a *pumpkin* is safe on Hallowe'en.

Victoria Woods (13)

CHANGING SEASONS

A winter's night, harsh and cold,
with the moon shining bright and bold.
Whilst stars sparkle in the darkened sky,
Can be heard the sound of an animal's cry.

As early light brings the morning,
a fresh new day is dawning.
Frozen rivers begin to flow
as the sun melts the glittering snow.

Glistening frost all around
descends in droplets to the ground,
forming puddles where they fall
welcoming the new season's call.

As wintertime fades away,
can be felt the warmth of a sunny day.
The bleating of lambs so young,
for springtime has begun.

The chorus of the early bird
singing sweetly can be heard.
While flowers and blossom start to bloom,
signals the end of winter's gloom.

Kirsty Birch (13)

World

The world is always tough,
Although it sometimes doesn't seem,
When you really try,
You might just get by.

When you feel really sad,
And things don't go your way,
Then you mustn't just give up,
You should laugh, play and say.

If nobody wants to see you,
Or if they don't want to play,
Then you should just ignore them,
And go your own way.

Donna Wheeler (13)

S S Titanic

A wonderful gleaming brand new ship,
Out to sail all seven blue seas.
Everyone had claimed her unsinkable,
If only they knew what was going to be.

S S Titanic would soon meet her fate,
The unsinkable ship destined to sink.
Who knew the Atlantic could be a grave,
To a wonderful gleaming brand new ship.

Jenny Norris (13)

HOMELESS

Feelin' lonely, feelin' down,
That's how I feel all year round.

Lying on the stone floor,
Making you feel sore,
People in their warm houses closing their door.
Stuck outside all year,
Seeing people going for a beer.

In the winter it's much worse,
The cold can make you feel cursed.

Sarah Coleman (13)

Before The Dawn

Before the dawn the world is still,
A dark blue rug across the land,
No birds are singing in the trees,
No hustle bustle of the town.

I long for sound and light and warmth,
For birds to sing a song,
Why is it the day is so short,
And yet the night so long?

Then the magic starts to happen,
A streak of light as day is born,
The first note from a waking world,
There is no more before the dawn.

Jessica Vallis (13)

ANGER

The IRA make me angry when they plant bombs,
they kill innocent people who are so young,
so much loss and so much pain,
surely it should never happen again.

Call a cease-fire and it will all stop,
the people of Great Britain will not have to worry,
no more violence, no more pain,
surely it should never happen again.

So could you please stop,
and the people of Ireland will be at peace again.

Mark Ilsley (14)

EVERYBODY IS EQUAL

Are we really different,
I think we're all the same.
It doesn't matter who you are,
You shouldn't be ashamed.
White, black or Asian, rich or poor,
Your outside makes no difference,
It's the inside that counts more.
Why are people careless?
They don't care who they hurt,
The victims end up feeling sad,
And it makes them feel like dirt.
Racism is pointless,
There is no point to prove,
Everyone is equal,
Therefore no one should lose.
Why do so many people
Let judgement rule their life?
It leaves the sufferers empty,
Their happiness is deprived.
So colour makes no difference,
It's just the way we're born,
Everyone's exactly the same
And will be forever more!

Elizabeth Marchant (13)

ANGER

My brother makes me angry when he annoys me,
But he's okay when he lends me his pocket money.
Dogs make me angry when they poo on the road,
But they're okay when they do a little not a load.

My parents can make me angry when they moan at me,
But they're okay 'cause they're often good to me.
Bad films annoy me when you watch them 'til the end,
Then you find out there's a rubbish end.

David Beckham annoyed me 'cause he cost us the World Cup,
But I think you should forgive him, everyone at some stage messes up.
I don't often get angry but when I do,
I scream and I shout, I often blow a fuse.

Daniel Henwood (14)

ABUSE

I look at the sky so blue,
and wonder why it happened to you.
Did you deserve it?
All the yelling and being hit.

You looked like you'd been to the war,
when you said you walked into a door.
Black and blue from bruising,
no way were you cruising.
You just sat and took it all.

That was a year ago now,
no longer you have those rows.
You didn't want anymore,
your parents are now in Broadmoor.
Everyone's got what they wanted,
although you're no longer here to want it.

After that fatal night,
when you were held real tight,
you lay in your grave,
so small and brave,
as you died from the accused,
Child abuse.

Lucy Cox (13)

SCHOOL

School is a funny place
Nowhere else has quite the same case
We all moan about school
But in a way it's quite cool
It is a chance to learn things new
The need for an education is true
Without it where would we be
There are not many possibilities
Nothing to talk about, no friends to meet
So in a way school is quite neat!

Emma Windiate (14)

The Bus

Waiting here in the rain,
Am I early again?
The bus is late again,
My friends have got here at last,
We start to talk about the past.
Fumble, fumble, where is my silly bus pass?
In the wind my coat flapped,
The bus looked really clapped out.
As we get on the bus we push
So there is a crush.
As we get on the bus the driver gave us friendly smiles,
We wish we could go miles and miles.
Now comes the time for real will,
I hope we do get up the hill.
Three at the back have gone bonkers
Playing with their conkers.
The ancient bus jolts and jumps
As it goes over the massive bumps.
I do believe the school is in sight,
Oh no they've started another fight.

Emma Porter (14)

DREAMS

I've always dreamt of flying high
Looking down from above in the sky
To race against the clouds soaring by
Oh how I wish that I could fly

I've always dreamt of travelling far
Whether it be by plane, ship or car
I've always dreamt of being a star
Watching the world from afar

I've always dreamt of a house in the sun
The worries of the world I would shun
Sitting back when my work is done
Then is the time I could have some fun.

Emma Perry (13)

FIREWORKS

F antastic colours ignite the blackened sky
I nfinitely popping and whizzing by
R ushing through the cold and the smoky air
E xploding through the meadow, crowds and fair
W hirling Catherine wheels bring gasps of delight
O range bonfire flames flicker through the night
R ockets whooshing high make a splendid array
K aleidoscope colours merge and spray
S parklers weave the children's names and end the display.

Shonagh Keddie (13)

The Seasons

Seasons come and seasons go,
Some bring sunshine some bring snow,
Summer, autumn, winter, spring,
With the first we shall begin.

Spring is when flowers start to appear,
From where you planted them last year,
Animals are coming out of hibernation,
Each one of them is God's creation.

Summer is a time when the sun does shine,
So people sit in their gardens drinking wine,
The birds start to reappear,
From where they flew to last year.

Autumn is a time when the leaves start to fall,
And the weather starts to turn cool,
Birds are preparing to fly away,
To a warmer place where they can stay.

Winter is the time of year,
When people buy presents, for Christmas is near,
Animals would have hibernated long ago,
To hide away from the freezing snow.

Joanne Stuart (13)

FOOD

F ood is mostly found in shops,
O ften in packets, often not.
O melettes, cheese, yoghurt and milk,
D airy products they taste like silk.

Food is important and very yummy,
and it digests in your tummy.

Charmain Vaughan (13)

OCEAN POEM

The coral reef shines very bright,
Oysters give off a pearly light,
There are many treasures in the sea,
That hide beneath a dark, dark lee.

Dolphins swim around and around,
They make the most beautiful sound,
Starfish and sea horses swim here,
The water is so crystal clear.

Colours of the coral are blue and green,
Tropical fish seem so keen,
They swim around with their friends,
And turn each little winding bend.

The sparkling ocean is like a magical potion,
As the sun sets on the bay,
It looks like the end of another day,
The moon will be up soon,
And shine on that special lagoon.

Tiffany Dale (13)

THE SEA

The sea, the sea, the wonderful sea
And I am sure it's the place for me.
The waves, the waves, the wonderful waves
They roll and turn and go gushing into caves.
The fish, the fish, the tropical fish
They swim and splash and splash and splish.
The seaweed, the seaweed it really smells
It floats on the floor and sticks to the shells.
The sea, the sea, the deep blue sea
I'm really sure it's the holiday for me.
It's crystal clear, it's crystal clear,
Come on everybody the sea is here.

Melanie Lanes (13)

FOOTBALL'S THE BEST!

Football's the best,
Better than all the rest.
The World Cup is cool,
Never a disappointment at all.

Back in old Blighty,
Football's played nightly.
The aim is to score,
Then you'll hear a roar.

When the Cups have been won,
Football has not gone.
There's still friendlies to play,
At home or away.

Playing international,
It is fantastical.
It's rewarded by a cap,
And the fans will all clap!

Football's the best,
Better than the rest!

Paul Seymour (14)

CHILD ABUSE

Imagine a room dark, black and cold,
You see a small child battered and in his mother's hold,
He screams, he bellows but no one can hear,
This is child abuse, remember his fear.

Imagine a garden, laden with flowers,
Then you see a mother, showing her powers,
You hear a little voice, then you see a little face,
Last of all you see a hand, it is raised, but you turn around in haste,
This is child abuse, remember his fear.

Imagine a bedroom, first thing in the morning,
You see a child rise and then you hear him yawning,
You hear a woman shouting 'Shut up that noise now'
Then you hear a scream and a smothering with a towel,
This is child abuse, remember his fear.

The only love he gave, thrown back in his face,
For what happens behind closed doors,
Only he had to endure,
This is child abuse, remember his fear,
remember his fear.

Debbie Hill (13)

WHO AM I?

I am a small part of the world,
Hidden away from most.
I am unknown to many,
But known to some.
I am a daughter, a friend and a sister.
I am a single soul,
Inside a single body.
I am part of an amazing jigsaw,
Without me the jigsaw is incomplete.
I am special, I am amazing,
I am a child of the world.

Charlotte Berger (13)

Bimble, The Billy Goat, The Bucket And The Thimble

There once was a bomble
A bomble named Bimble
Bimble had a bucket
In which he had a thimble.
Bimble also had a billy goat,
Which had a very strong throat.
They got into their boat
And set themselves afloat.

Now Bimble and his billy goat
Which, by the way, had a very strong throat,
Noticed that their boat
Was no longer afloat!

So into the bucket climbed Bimble,
And the goat got into the thimble,
But as their boat went under,
They made a bit of a blunder,
And forgot to grab the oar,
So now they are no more!

Poor little Bimble,
Poor little goat,
Which, by the way, had a very strong throat,
Poor little bucket,
Poor little thimble,
Yes, that was the end of lovely old Bimble.

Amy Fowler (12)

PAIN, RELIEF, CONSEQUENCES

A muddle of faces and voices.
A pounding hurting feeling.
Desperate not knowing what to do.
Pain never ceasing always there.
Looking for a place to go, to hide.
Anger tearing a frantic, lunatic raging inside me.
Trying to control myself.
Stepping out of real life and into a dream.

Then as if by magic my pain is relieved.
I'd done it, I try again and it helps me.
The pain flows out in rivers and eases me.
Then I can't do it, the craziness returns.
I look for anything to cease the pain.

Then I stop. I feel scared.
But I look thoughtfully at what I have done.
And I'm shocked; but the pain has gone.
It's been washed away like sand in the waves.
But then comes the trembling and terror.
What if someone sees or just knows.
But I calm myself and look at what I've done
It was an instant painkiller.

Susan McCauley (13)

Fulfilled Hope

The bright golden sun emerges
From the hillside
The rays rush down the valley
To a child
He walks towards the light
Dawdling, wearily.
His eyes brighten at the sight
Of the birth of new hope
He has found what he was looking for
His dream is now fulfilled
The frontier has been crossed.

Kate Walley (12)

A Star

I sing of a star,
The sun and the moon.

I sing of the planets,
Of Mars and Neptune.

I sing of the other stars,
The sparkling suns,

I sing of America,
Of Bosnia and guns.

I sing of the sky,
The Heavens above,

I sing of the Lord,
Of Jesus and love.

I sing of myself,
Flying high.

I sing of myself,
Up in the sky.

Sarah Johnstone (13)

Survival

A hungry, small, weak child
In torn clothes
His face tired and afraid
Of being alone
Staggered desperately away
From the squat
With no hope and no food
And no home
In a continuing attempt
To survive
On his own in the world.

Isabel Sibley (13)

My Definition Of Poetry

Poetry is like wind -
always there, but not always seen.
Poetry is like the weather -
changing as time moves on.
Poetry is like a black hole -
never ending.
Poetry is like a letter -
packed with information.
Poetry is like maths -
difficult to understand at first.
Poetry is like a drum -
beating out a warning.
Poetry is like a flame -
giving a feeling of warmth.
Poetry is like a picture -
interpreted in all different ways.
Poetry is a part of us.

Rachel Geneen (13)

Old Man

A wise old man sits in the station
without a worry in the world.
He just sits there sipping his tea.
His big brown eyes peer over his glasses.
He's looking at the people around him.
Is he alone?
No, he's with his wife
sitting there, dreaming.

His feet are tapping the ground
His burgundy jacket wrapped around him
The collar button of his dull pink shirt
Is undone
No tie
No briefcase
Going away on a train?
Up he gets and trots away
His wife following closely behind him.

Jenna Ward (13)

Herbs In Our Garden

The herbs in the garden
Are never in a rush,
They sway in their patches,
And sway in the crush.

The plants called curry,
Smell so sweet,
Chives are very useful,
And good to eat.

There are many herbs in the garden,
Lavender, dill and thyme,
Come to our herb garden,
And have a good time!

Zoe Osborne (12)

Herb Life

They creep high, they creep low,
Tangle within themselves
Like people to and fro.
They send out aroma,
Making themselves known,
They creep back in,
From night to dawn.
When morning returns
They regain their life.
Send out misty odours
And bring back life.
Bees and insects smother the leaves
Trying to regain their patch for the week.
People brush past,
Stamping over the hyssop and Rosemary too
But also opening up a new era.
Brand new lavender and dill appears
And once more,
It starts again.
They'll creep high, they'll creep low
Tangle within themselves
Like people to and fro.

Parveen Sohal (15)

The Frozen Town

The children skate, old people too.
Men from the hunt are tired with no food for tonight.
The dogs lag behind - cold and sad,
Unsatisfied by the work they have done.

The little girl standing by the fire feels its warmth,
As the birds watch over the town
In the dusky light.
White snow freshly laid covers the tops
Of houses and ground.

The creaking inn sign disturbs no one.
The hunters are cold but
The skaters seem warm
In their hearts, at least,
As they play before they rest.

Tracy Taylor (17)

My Secret

I have a secret to tell
I'll tell you
If you don't tell anyone.

It's about a boy
You are my best friend
Promise me you won't tell.

This secret goes beyond
My heart thumping down below.
If you tell my heart will split.

This secret is between you and me
And is about someone
If you let it slip
You will soon feel
The blue icy breath of
Death!

Selina Sayers (12)

FRIENDSHIP

Making friends isn't an easy thing,
You can't make them like being a king,
Things are needed like love, respect and trust,
So you see racism and cruelty isn't the recipe
For falling in love.

    There is nothing like a good friend in the world
    He or she goes through bad times and good times with you.

Friends are people you like, love, trust and respect,
  even if they could infect.
Friends are those you play with happily.
You might just have a few quarrels but that's just because
  you love them so much.
But you must always remember to love them very much.

Monaza Sheikh (13)

Bubbles

I blow some bubbles
And they float away,
Into the sky.
They are big and small,
They rise and fall.
I watch them
Glistening in the sun.
All the colours of the rainbow
Until . . .
Pop!

Mikaela Shelton (12)

DIANA

D iana is now an angel
I n Heaven she shall remain
A lways watching over us
N ever to be seen again
A nd all our lives depend on her,
for she was the chosen one.

Zara Stacey (13)

My World!

My world,
No one *knows* me in my
world,
No one *sees* me in my
world,
All they see is me
With my blondish
hair,
With my bluish
eyes
In my weirdish way.

It's a disguise!

Claire Tickner (12)

ANIMALS

I love animals, especially whales,
They are mammals, not fish with scales.
Lions, tigers, hippos too
If you want to see them, go to a zoo.
Fish and frogs
Visit a pond.
What can I have for a pet?
What do I want?

Donna Waters (12)

FRIENDS

One of the most important things in your life are your friends.
This is because friendships never end!
When you're unhappy or sad,
or even angry or mad,
you should be glad,
that your friends are your friends!

You could talk to them on the phone
or even visit them at home,
and you will always know that your friends aren't your foe.
When you shed a tear,
your friends will be near.
My friends would run a mile
just to see me smile!

I would just like to say
that my friends always make my day!

Danielle Willmott (13)

Family

F aith and trust in your family.
A rguments go on in families, some worse than others.
M y family make decisions together.
I would do anything for my family.
L ove and caring goes on in a family.
Y ou get independence from your family.

Rebekah Wilson (12)

The Tiger!

The tiger is a sleepy cat
wandering all around the jungle.

He roars around his throne
and has no care in the world.

The tiger is like a black and yellow
striped bee, who waits for his prey,
prowls for his dinner.

But, before that, his evil enemies arrive!

The tiger makes his last speech.
'I'd better watch out,
or I'll become a lady's fashionable coat!'

Hajira Naveed (13)

On a Cold Winter's Day

There was a great crash of waves,
as the wind swept up and upon the sea

The wind was roaring, screaming,
a pain so deep as a lost love.

The ground swept up the falling leaves
and reached for the branches enticingly.

The people shivered in their warmless homes
only daring to move when there was food to eat.
No homely feel was there about these homes,
or love between the world and others.

Keren Otto (12)

Isn't It Weird

Isn't it weird there's more than one star!
Isn't it weird that a planet is named after a Mars bar!
Isn't it weird that a train's always late!
Isn't it weird that it's hard to make mates!
Isn't it weird that everything is weird in life!

Leanne Price (12)

My Poem

I like puppy dogs but
I don't like slimy frogs.
I like swimming but
I don't like nattering women.
I like fluffy cats but
I don't like black bats.
I like playing pool but
I don't like school.
I like pearls but
I don't like naughty girls.
I like climbing rocks but
I don't like smelly socks.

Claire Brooks (12)

My Likes And Dislikes

I like some teachers but not all,
I dislike brothers and sisters especially small.
I love my mum and dad,
and I like my friends 'cos when I'm with them,
fun never ends.
I like Five but not Boyzone.
I like being away
but prefer it at home.
I like history, don't like Latin,
don't mind cotton but I prefer satin.
I like blue, don't like pink,
and I don't like homework
because you need to think.

Tracey Carr (12)

Likes And Loves

I love the grass,
so soft and green.
I'd love my room
if it was clean.
I love going out
on hot days,
but love staying in
and having a laze.
I love going shopping
in the town mall
but I love having fun
that's the best of all.

Rachel Fisher (12)

My Poem

I like singing and dancing
I like chocolate ice-cream
I like watching TV
I always watch Rugrats.

But I don't like spiders,
and I don't like wasps.
I don't like toads
and I don't like frogs.

Sammy-Jo Haines (12)

LIKES AND DISLIKES

I don't like racism
because we're all the same
I don't like Latin
Isn't that a shame

I like swimming only
when it's warm
I don't like the dark
and I don't like storms

I don't like the cold
I like it when it's sunny
I like going shopping
if it's someone else's money.

Carina Hill (12)

Grumpy Babies

Babies are grumpy when
they have wind,
they're grumpy with a dirty nappy,
'pooh' put it in the bin.

Babies are happy when
they have had their food,
but after that comes
something quite crude!

I love babies especially
when they're asleep,
so I can sit and relax
and have something to eat.

Catherine Igoe (12)

Street Child

Little street child all alone,
daydreaming all day,
finding out what he can.
Shoe-shining gets his pay;
left to rot in the streets,
the leftovers are what he eats.

Little street child,
keep your spirits high,
do not worry,
we will help you,
someday, somehow.

Samantha Mackie (12)

BEARS

I like bears they are so sweet,
with big, big paws and big, big feet.
Koala bears, they are the best,
bears have a cave and not a nest.
They eat the berries from the woods,
they have thick fur, not coats with hoods.
I would like to be a bear,
with long, sharp claws and thick, brown hair.
But I'm a human, plain as can be,
and I'm happy just being me!

Charmaine McCully (13)